50 SIMPLE INDOOR
MINIATURE
GARDENS

Publication management
Isabelle Jeuge-Maynart & Ghislaine Stora

Chief editor
Catherine Delprat

Editing and coordination
Agnès Dumoussaud

Graphic design
Aurore Elie

Layout
J²Graph/Jacqueline Gensollen-Bloch

Production
Donia Faiz

English translation
Ulatus

English edition editing
Colleen Dorsey

English edition design
Wendy Reynolds

Cover photo: © GAP Photos/Visions.

ISBN 978-1-4971-0048-0

The Cataloging-in-Publication Data is on file with the Library of Congress.

To learn more about the other great books from Fox Chapel Publishing, or to find a retailer near you, call toll-free 800-457-9112 or visit us at *www.FoxChapelPublishing.com*.

We are always looking for talented authors. To submit an idea, please send a brief inquiry to acquisitions@foxchapelpublishing.com.

Printed in China
First printing

Because working with plants and other materials inherently includes the risk of injury and damage, this book cannot guarantee that creating the projects in this book is safe for everyone. For this reason, this book is sold without warranties or guarantees of any kind, expressed or implied, and the publisher and the author disclaim any liability for any injuries, losses, or damages caused in any way by the content of this book or the reader's use of the tools needed to complete the projects presented here. The publisher and the author urge all readers to thoroughly review each project and to understand the use of all tools before beginning any project.

50 SIMPLE INDOOR MINIATURE GARDENS

DECORATING YOUR HOME WITH INDOOR PLANTS

CATHERINE DELVAUX

Fox Chapel
PUBLISHING

CONTENTS

THE ESSENTIALS

The keys to successful arrangements............................ 12

Choosing the right plants to buy................................ 14

Choosing the right pots and tools.............................. 16

The right soil 18

Finding the perfect spot 20

Rules for planting... 22

Daily care 24

10 essential cacti and succulents 28

10 essential indoor plants..................................... 30

TERRARIUMS AND KOKEDAMAS

Creating a mini-forest from scratch 34

Mini-greenhouses 36

A small echeveria in a jar..................................... 38

A nature corner in your house 40

Creating a green and white flowerbed.......................... 42

An air plant display... 44

A cupful of greenery... 46

The Mexican desert in a jar 48

Air plants take flight... 50

Lightweight hanging planters 52

The perfect kokedama for beginners 54

Orchid kokedama 56

Succulent kokedamas 58

GREEN WALLS

Spring forecast 62

A daring cactus shelf. 64

Strawberries on every shelf. 66

A little primrose theater 68

Creating a stunning floral wall 70

Repurposing vintage objects. 72

A living wall of air plants. 74

A botanical birdhouse 76

Primroses growing in a sieve 78

A living wall of lettuce 80

CREATIVE CONTAINERS

Putting spring in boxes 84

A "leek"-ing teapot 86

Breathe in the seaside air 88

Succulents striking a pose. 90

Lovely lobelias in a row 92

Strange-looking hermit crabs 94

Spring comes early 96

Funny-looking olives 98

Mineral-enhanced plant 100

Venture off the beaten path 102

Ferns, a piece of cake!. 104

Hyacinths are in!. 106

A succulent gift basket. 108

A little taste of summer on your window. 110

Hyacinths in a box. 112

Succulent upholstery 114

POTS AND PLANTERS

Treat yourself to some springtime sweets 118

Orange is the new green 120

A waterfall of green. 122

Traveling to hot climates. 124

In life, there are cacti 126

A neat manicure for your snake plant 128

An adorable dry mini-garden 130

Moss up your décor!. 132

A lovely collection of cacti 134

Nasturtiums get a makeover 136

Simply easy succulents. 138

    Plant index 140

    Image credits 142

    About the author. 144

FOREWORD

Green décor is on the rise: the tiniest windowsills are now covered in plant life. Our houses are not far behind: they host original terrariums, mini vegetable gardens, hanging gardens, and unique arrangements. These little green touches in every room of the house and out on terraces and balconies are trendy and refreshing. You can create a small relaxing oasis, stage an indoor garden, or simply display your green creations.

The one thing all these ideas have in common is that they are simple to create and their upkeep is often minimal. Plants are timeless, making them a virtual guarantee of success no matter your personal style. All the different plants presented in this book can be easily found in large garden centers, and many can be acquired from local fellow gardeners (sedum rosettes, different echeveria species, cuttings of spider plant, discarded strawberry plants, a piece of helxine divided from a large clump...).

Plant containers, on the other hand, are undergoing a revolution: long gone is the age of the basic terracotta pot. We can recycle, repair, transform, and repurpose run-of-the-mill objects to create new and interesting homes for plants. Anything is possible— all you have to do is imagine it! Whether you prefer cacti, succulents, vegetables, green plants, or flowering plants, these 50 inspirational arrangements, quirky and totally contemporary, will awaken the creative gardener inside you.

THE ESSENTIALS

The arrangements that are presented to you in this book are only guidelines; you don't need to follow the instructions to the letter. If you can't find the exact species or variety, it doesn't matter. Just stick to the major plant categories: replace one cactus with another, one air plant with another (if necessary, ask a salesperson for advice). Most similar plants' needs are exactly the same, and they will grow in the same way.

THE KEYS TO SUCCESSFUL ARRANGEMENTS

THE ARRANGEMENTS PRESENTED HERE VARY SIGNIFICANTLY. SOME NEED TO BE SET UP OUTSIDE, IN THE GARDEN, ON A BALCONY OR TERRACE, OR EVEN ON YOUR WINDOWSILL. OTHERS SHOULD ONLY BE SET UP INSIDE. STILL OTHERS SHOULD BE KEPT INSIDE DURING WINTER AND MOVED OUTSIDE IN SUMMER.

Outdoor planters

Winter or early spring plants (pansies, bulbs, primroses, etc.) are available very early in garden centers. They have been grown in greenhouses: if you plant them outside without any transition period and it's cold, they will not survive. But they should not be kept inside where it is too warm and dry. The best thing to do is to place them against the house, where they will be sheltered and kept warmer. If at night the temperature drops below freezing, you should bring them inside in the basement or garage and put them back out the next day. It's a little bit frustrating at the beginning, but it's the only way to keep them alive and see them bloom over time.

For summer plants (pelargoniums, petunias, verbenias, lobelias, etc.), wait until after the temperatures consistently stay above freezing before placing them outside. This is usally by mid-May, but you should know the climate where you live to make sure there is no longer any risk of freezing, even at night.

Follow this useful advice:
• Do not plant seasonal plants too far apart, as they bloom quickly and do not last long.

• Pay attention to the weight of your larger planters. Make lighter soil blends by replacing one third of the soil with vermiculite. This way you can reduce the total weight by about one third.

Potted plants on windowsills

Use common sense when deciding placement.
• Make sure that the base of the pot is not wider than the windowsill.
• Make sure the pots can't tip over.
• Check that the pots do not prevent the shutters from closing.
• Make sure that you can easily reach the pots to water and take care of them.
• Avoid planters less than 6" (15cm) in diameter, as you will have to water them more often due to a lack of soil.
• Avoid plants that grow too tall or too wide. They will quickly stifle the other plants and block the light inside the house.

Indoor arrangements

The rules are more or less the same as for outdoor pots, with some additional constraints.
• Place large plates underneath the pots so as not to wet the floor or furniture.
• Do not place pots in heavily trafficked walkways, as the foliage will get damaged.

Hanging plants

Pay close attention to the following points.
• Make sure that the wires are strong enough to support the weight. Keep in mind that wet soil weighs up to a third more than dry soil.
• Don't place hanging plants in drafty or windy areas.
• Make sure that you can easily reach the arrangements to water them.

Terrariums

Terrariums were originally popularized by the Victorians. After going out of fashion for many years, people regained interest in them in the 1980s, with the famous "dame-jeanne," bulky glass cylinders. Then they fell out of style again before experiencing a resurgence in the form of containers with interesting shapes (like tube vases), repurposed jars, decorative glass bells, and minimalist mini-terrariums with just one or two plants. If a terrarium is equipped with a cap or lid, it creates a closed system that can be self-sufficient for many weeks. If it is left open, it creates a mini-greenhouse.
• If you have little light, opt for a closed system, suitable for undergrowth or tropical plants, which thrive with warmth, shade, and moisture.
• If you have a lot of sun, go for an open system with cacti and succulents, which will appreciate the warmth and brightness.

CHOOSING THE RIGHT PLANTS TO BUY

GARDEN CENTERS USUALLY HAVE AN ABUNDANCE OF CHOICES, AND THE PRICES ARE USUALLY FAIR. BUT DO NOT FORGET THAT THERE ARE ALSO PROFESSIONALS WHO WILL ALWAYS WELCOME YOU INTO THEIR PLACE OF PRODUCTION: PLANT NURSERIES. YOU CAN ALSO FIND A LOT OF SPECIALISTS ON THE INTERNET.

SOWING OR PLANTING?

This is a good question for some of the plants used in the arrangements in this book, such as **nasturtiums, lettuce, and parsley.** It obviously depends on when you buy them. For lettuce and parsley, if you are a beginner, buy them as plants; they will grow quicker and stronger. Nasturtiums are more difficult to grow and only last a short while (the stems are fragile, and they are often left for too long in stores). On the other hand, their big seeds are easy to sow and grow quickly. So buy a packet of seeds instead.

For **bulbs,** such as hyacinths or snowdrops, is it better to buy bulbs in autumn, prepare the arrangement or pots of bulbs, leave them outside in the winter, and return to them in the spring when the shoots come out, or to buy growing plants in the spring? Both ways of doing things are relatively easy. Be aware that for the same budget, you can buy more bulbs in the fall than you can buy pre-cultivated, potted plants in the spring.

At the garden center

Garden centers usually stock up for the weekend: ask the manager of yours when the deliveries come in, as it is often **Thursday** or **Friday.** The stock is regularly rotated, and the plants are maintained by professionals and stored in places that are suitable for them. You can choose from a range of sizes and species and check whether the plant is flowering and if that flower is the right color.

For **bigger specimens,** check if their roots fill the pot. If you can, flip the plant over and take the root ball out of the pot entirely. If the earth crumbles, it has been repotted recently; if, on the other hand, the roots line the bottom of the pot and wrap around the walls, the plant will need to be repotted. The ideal scenario is a compact mound with vigorous, healthy roots that have not yet filled the pot. The part of the plant above the soil should be balanced, bushy but not too bushy, and healthy.

For **smaller specimens** (potted cacti, small plants), the problems that affect bigger plants don't tend to arise because the plants are still young.

If it's cold outside, transport your plants properly. This is especially important for orchids, which cannot withstand a cold snap (several hours in an unheated car while it's freezing outside, for example): the buds will fall off. Even on a short ride, remember that if the plants are more tightly packaged, they will travel better, breaking less. Bring along some newspaper to wrap them in, just in case there isn't any at the checkout counter.

At a specialized nursery

The specialists at plant nuseries know their plants inside and out and can give you valuable advice if you are buying on the spot. You can also order plants from them through the mail. Some nurseries sell rare species that are difficult to find elsewhere, and many have extensive collections (including cacti and succulents, orchids, air plants, and more).

On the Internet

Online, the range of plants available is virtually unlimited, but sometimes they are sold by resellers and you do not necessarily have a

guarantee that the product is what they say it is or that it will be in good condition when it arrives, especially if it is coming from abroad. If it is the first time you've ordered something from a particular site, only order a few items. If all goes well (ordering, delivery times, careful packaging, quality and freshness of plants, correct species and varieties as requested, etc.), you can then make larger orders.

In large grocery stores or craft stores

Big-box grocery and craft stores often sell cacti and annual/seasonal bulbs at attractive prices. But are these good-quality plants? Only your wisdom and keen eye will be able to answer that question. A low price does not necessarily mean the plants are of poor quality. This is also the case with garden center promotions. Check to see if the plants are healthy, if they have flower buds and solid shoots. A faded flower or a broken branch should not stop you if the rest of the plant looks healthy and vigorous.

CHOOSING THE RIGHT POTS AND TOOLS

IF YOU HAVE TO CHOOSE A POT FOR AN ARRANGEMENT, DO NOT BUY AT RANDOM: NOT ALL POTS ARE MADE EQUAL. THE SAME GOES FOR BUYING TOOLS: BE SURE TO BUY QUALITY TOOLS, BECAUSE THEY WILL WORK BETTER AND LAST LONGER, AND THEIR PARTS CAN BE REPLACED.

Pot materials

• **Different decorative containers** (wooden boxes, cans, cups, etc.) are not necessarily suitable for planting: they have no holes for draining water. If you can puncture a hole in them without breaking the container, then we recommend that you do just that. If not, consider putting a layer of clay balls at the bottom and isolating the roots with a piece of nonwoven textile or drainage felt. This will absorb the water and prevent it from building up and going stagnant.

• **Plastic pots** are light, malleable, cheap, and come in a wide range of shapes and colors. You can also hide plastic pots in prettier flowerpots.

• **Terracotta:** under the umbrella term "pottery," there is a wide range of products of varying quality. If you want to use a terracotta or other pottery product outside, check the manufacturer's guarantee regarding its frost resistance.

• **Fiberglass pots** are lightweight and are available in attractive, modern shapes.

• **Zinc,** whose appearance changes over time, has a more vintage feel.

• **Wooden planters** are decorative but have little resistance to moisture on the outside and are quite heavy (physically and aesthetically).

What size pot should you choose?

If it is small, ephemeral arrangements that you want, the size of the container matters very little. You will have to replant in a larger pot after a few weeks. This is not the case if you want a long-lasting arrangement.

• **Width (diameter):** A container with a width of less than 4" (10cm) is too narrow. A width of 6" to 8" (15 to 20cm) gives the plant room to grow and is less likely to dry out.

• **Depth:** Very few plants can thrive in pots that are only 2" (5cm) deep. Even cacti, which usually come in tiny pots, still need at least 4" (10cm) to grow properly. Don't forget that in nature these plants grow long roots that reach deep into the ground to find water!

Tools

• **A pair of pruning shears** is the most essential tool in a gardener's arsenal. Do not skimp on the quality. Even if you do not intend to cut thick branches, nothing is more frustrating than a tool that is difficult to hold, is stiff to open and close, and hacks up the plant. For small arrangements, choose a model with thin blades or scissors that can cut anything; these are the most practical shears. Test out any pruning shears before buying them, because there are shears for all hand sizes as well as for right- and left-handed people. Some shears are also heavier than others.

It is important to measure you own hands first with a ruler to get a better idea of what size you will need. Lay your hand flat, fingers together, and measure the width of your hand at the widest point. A measurement less than 3½" (8.5cm) corresponds to size small (S); between 3½" and 4" (8.5 and 10cm), size medium (M); and greater than 4" (10cm), size large (L). If you are between

two sizes, choose the smaller one, as these will be more comfortable to work with.

• **A dibber or dibbler** is a must-have. This pointed stick allows you to dig a small hole in the ground to plant seeds, pack potting soil, and mix other ingredients with soil.

• **Soil shovels** allow you to mix different substrates without dirtying your hands.

• **A plastic tarpaulin** is essential if you plan to do any gardening work inside your apartment or home. It will allow you to repot plants without making a mess or needing to lay newspaper everywhere.

• **A plastic or zinc basin** is recommended for city gardeners. If you have a large enough basin, you can repot plants without dirtying your surroundings. You can mix potting soil, sand, vermiculite, and clay balls in it. You can also store bags of different soil types in it. It can be moved and stored easily.

THE RIGHT SOIL

IN A POT, SOIL IS SUBJECT TO CONSTRAINTS THAT DO NOT EXIST IN NATURE. IT MUST NOT, AMONG OTHER THINGS, GET BOGGED DOWN BY BEING WATERED TOO FREQUENTLY. YOU CAN IMPROVE THE QUALITY OF THE SUBSTRATES BY MAKING YOUR OWN MIXES.

For potted plants

The number one danger, which goes hand in hand with dry soil, is **root suffocation.** Roots need water, but they also need air. When the soil settles after repeated watering, the air inside the soil escapes. This makes it difficult for the roots to breathe. A part of the root dies, making it difficult for the water to drain. Thus begins a vicious circle! Before planting, to check whether the soil is well ventilated, press it into the hollow of your hand: if it crumbles into small pieces, then it is well ventilated.

Use potting soils for all your plants, never soil collected from nature. Potting soils used for geraniums, planters, and potted plants are a good starting point, as they contain materials that do not settle (perlite, for example). You can also improve the quality of the soil: add 4¼ cups (1L) of perlite and 4¼ cups (1L) of pozzolana or small clay balls to 9 dry quarts / 42 cups (10L) of potting soil. These aerated and incompressible materials will help maintain the quality of the soil even after repeated watering. The richness of the soil is a secondary factor, since you can add fertilizer at any time.

For cacti and succulents

The issue of root suffocation does not arise for cacti and succulents: the soils for cacti contain a good proportion of sand, which does not compress easily. These plants also don't need watering as much, so there is a minimal risk of the soil settling. If you do not have potting soil for cacti on hand, you can make it yourself: add 1¾ dry quarts / 8½ cups (2L) of not-too-fine sand (this can be found in aquarium shops) and 4¼ cups (1L) of perlite or clay balls to 4½ dry quarts / 21 cups (5L) of standard potting soil (for your average green plants).

CHARCOAL, A MIRACLE PRODUCT

Everyone is aware of charcoal, which is wood that hasn't been completely burnt (completely burnt wood turns to ash). It has a very porous structure that gives it absorbent properties: it has the ability to prevent and therefore neutralize microscopic bacteria and fungi growth.

It works wonders in gardens: you can soak the base of cacti and succulent cuttings in charcoal powder to accelerate healing. You can also prevent damping-off (where a fungus can kill seedlings in less than 24 hours) by sprinkling the surface of the substrate with a little bit of charcoal dust. It also prevents orchid rot. Just add pieces of charcoal to the growth medium. However, it is especially effective in preventing bacterial build-up that can lead to bad odors in terrariums. Place a few pieces of charcoal in the soil or sprinkle the base of the terrarium with charcoal dust.

It doesn't matter what type of charcoal you use, they all have the same effect. However, you should avoid using barbecuing charcoal because it has usually been treated (to make it more flammable). It is better to buy **horticultural charcoal** at a garden center, in pieces or as a powder. You can also make your own charcoal by recovering half-burnt pieces of wood from the ashes of a chimney or stove. Sort the solid, black pieces from the light and slightly brittle ones. If you want to make charcoal powder, simply take the pieces, put them in a mortar, and grind them into dust. Or put them in a plastic bag and crush them with a rolling pin or a hammer.

For closed terrariums

Take a standard potting soil and add 1 teaspoon of finely chopped charcoal per 4¼ cups (1L) of soil. This will prevent the growth of unwanted bacteria and fungi.

For vegetables

Vegetables need rich soil. Even commercial potting soil that already contains fertilizer will become depleted after a month of cultivation. You will reap nothing (or not much), and you definitely won't get long-lasting results (crops that can be harvested for more than 4 months) without fertilizer. Choose an organic fertilizer that should be administered every 2 weeks, or a fertilizer with delayed diffusion that is applied every 2 or 3 months.

For kokedamas

You can buy ready-to-use kokedama soil from the Internet, as there are still very few stores selling kokedamas and supplies even in major cities. Alternatively, you can make it yourself by mixing clay (found in craft stores), which you should allow to soak in water overnight, standard potting soil, and sphagnum/peat moss (found in small bags in the orchid section or near the substrates at your garden center). Grind it up a little before mixing it. Use equal parts of each material for the mix.

FINDING THE PERFECT SPOT

IT IS ALWAYS DIFFICULT TO CHOOSE WHERE IN A HOUSE
IS THE BEST PLACE FOR YOUR PLANTS. THROUGHOUT THE
YEAR, THE LIGHT CHANGES AROUND THE HOUSE. A SUITABLE
LOCATION IN WINTER MAY NOT BE SUITABLE IN SUMMER.

Where to place indoor plants

As you walk away from windows, the light intensity decreases rapidly. Math can explain this phenomenon: the luminosity decreases exponentially the further away you get from a window. In specific terms, a plant placed just 6½ ft. (2m) from a window will receive 4 times less light than one placed next to the window.

Of course, not all windows are equal: a window facing south is much brighter than a window facing east or west, and a lot brighter than one facing north (in the Northern hemisphere, that is). So you can move plants further away from a south-facing window than you can a north-facing one: 10 to 13 ft. (3 to 4m) in the first example, 3 to 6½ ft. (1 to 2m) in the second.

If you live in a city, then you may not get enough light. Place mirrors around the edges of your windows to reflect more light inside.

To further complicate the issue, each type of plant is different. Even within plant families (ferns, for example), some species will prefer the shade and others will need the sun. But whatever type of plant you choose, make sure that the leaves don't come into contact with cold windowpanes.

How do you know when a plant isn't in the right place?

You can tell just by looking. (Successful gardeners are usually said to have "green thumbs," but perhaps "green eyes" would be more appropriate!)

PLANTS STUCK IN THE SHADE
• The plant begins to wither; it continues growing upward, but its stems become thinner.
• The leaves are less green (the variegated varieties lose their variegation) and become stunted.
• The internodes become abnormally elongated.
• The plant grows poorly, and some leaves, particularly the lower ones, fall off.
• The plant leans toward the light source.
• The flowers are stunted or don't bloom at all.

What should you do? Place the plant nearer to the window or invest in an artificial light source.

PLANTS GETTING TOO MUCH SUN

• The plant looks "crispy."
• Its growth is slower; the edges of the leaves start to turn brown.
• The leaves are deformed and curled up.

What should you do? Move the plant away from the window; block the light in summer (with a curtain or blind). Cut off the burnt parts of the plant with scissors.

Every plant has its place

• **Moth orchids,** contrary to popular belief, don't like direct sunlight. They flower best when they've never seen a ray of sunlight. However, they do not do well when subject to air currents. If they are too cold, they refuse to flower or their buds drop off.
• **Cacti and succulents** like direct sunlight, but it is best not to leave them exposed in the window directly in the midday sun. They also don't like very cold rooms in winter. If they have to spend the winter in an unheated porch, water them less to allow them to bear the cold better. You should only water them when you see the foliage start to wither a little. All enjoy spending the summer outside, under the front porch for example, on the terrace, or on a windowsill.

• **For short-lived** potted plants (snowdrops, hyacinths, primroses, etc.), brightness does not matter much, because you will need to repot them in the garden when they have lost their flowers.
• **For kokedamas,** it depends on the plant, but it is better to avoid drafts, as they will dry out the moss covering.

WHAT IF YOU HAVE A DARK OR WINDOWLESS ROOM?

You can grow plants under an artificial light source. All you need to do is install a lamp of a suitable light type. Manufacturers and retailers use many different names for these: horticultural lamps, lighting bars, indoor plant lamps, growth lamps, etc. You can find them at any garden center. These lamps usually come in a kit including a lampshade with a reflector, a CFL (compact fluorescent lamp) bulb, and a switch. They should be turned on for 9 to 12 hours a day. Set up the plants so that their tips are about 12" to 35" (30 to 90cm) from the bulb.

One or two neon tubes (traditional or horticultural) are an alternative to these lamps, but they look out of place in a living room. There are also HPS (high-pressure sodium) lamps and metal-halide (MH) lamps. They are expensive and energy-consuming but good for professional gardeners.

RULES FOR PLANTING

THE AMOUNT OF CARE THAT YOU WILL TAKE WHEN PLANTING WILL DEPEND ON THE AESTHETIC OF THE ARRANGEMENT, THE LIFE EXPECTANCY OF THE PLANTS, AND HOW LONG THE PLANTS BLOOM. THERE ARE DIFFERENT RULES FOR DIFFERENT PLANT TYPES.

For green plants and flowers

1. Spread a 1" (2 to 3cm) thick drainage layer on the bottom of the pot, add some charcoal if needed, and then lay down a piece of drainage felt to insulate the roots from the drainage layer. Fill the pot halfway with potting soil.

2. Place the plants in the container (always moisten the roots beforehand by dipping them in water for a few minutes). The crown (the thin zone between the roots and stems) should be about 1½" (4cm) below the rim of the pot and be at the surface of the potting soil. If necessary, keep adding soil until it reaches the right level.

3. Add the potting soil by pressing/compacting it with your fingertips so that it adheres to the roots and no air pockets are formed. Press it well against the walls of the container too; this will keep the plant securely in place.

4. Water abundantly after planting, pouring the water gently so as not to displace the soil or uncover the roots. If necessary, add some more soil to fill in any gaps.

5. Cover the soil at the base of the plant with a protective mulch to minimize evaporation. For plants placed outside against a window, the mulch will prevent the rain from bouncing dirt onto the windows.

For orchids

1. Start by rinsing the orchid potting soil in a colander under clean water. Because the soil is chemically treated during its manufacture, it contains a lot of fine particles and dust that, once wet, will absorb too much water and may damage the orchid's roots. Remember that in nature orchids are epiphytic plants, meaning their roots are out in the open air on the branches of trees.

2. Remove the orchid from its pot and prune all dry, damaged, or rotted roots.

3. Put the plant into its new pot with pieces of bark between the roots. Use a small stake or dibber to completely fill in the gaps and compact the soil. The roots should be held firmly in place. Ideally, when repotting is complete, you should be able to lift up the orchid by the leaves without the pot and substrate falling off.

4. There is no need to water again, since you already wet the substrate at the start.

For kokedamas

1. Dilute the clay overnight with a little water to obtain a spreadable consistency.

2. Prepare the plant by removing it from its pot, then carefully removing the potting soil around the roots (possibly using a dibber) and cutting off one third of the roots. In the end, the mass of roots should be proportionate to the plant; this will create the best kokedama effect. You will have to judge for yourself how much you'll need to cut back to make it look well balanced.

3. Holding the plant with one hand, gradually add kokedama soil first between the roots and then all around to form a well-rounded ball, a little smaller than the desired final size.

4. Then place the moss all around the ball and tie everything together with three rounds of string. Use scissors to cut away any loose pieces of moss.

5. Gently water the kokedama, pouring a thin stream of water all over the ball.

For terrariums

1. Along the bottom of the container, spread a layer of clay balls or gravel 1" to 1½" (2 to 4cm) deep, which will act as a kind of "water tank." Spread a thin layer of charcoal on top.

2. Cover this with a piece of drainage felt (or non-woven fabric) so that the potting soil does not spill out. Spread another thin layer of charcoal on top.

3. Next, add a potting soil suitable for your plants (cacti potting soil and sand for succulents, potting soil mixed with perlite for flowering plants or vermiculite for moist plants). The soil and the drainage layer must occupy between one third and one half of the height of the terrarium; the rest is for the plants.

4. Finally, place the plants, making sure to give them enough room for air to circulate. Remember that the ratio of empty space in a terrarium is aesthetically very important. If a terrarium is too crowded, it doesn't look right. Then place any desired decorative elements in the terrarium (pebbles, branches, bark, etc.).

DAILY CARE

THE AMOUNT OF CARE REQUIRED WILL DEPEND ON THE TYPE OF PLANT. THERE ARE UNFORTUNATELY NO FIXED WATERING RULES TO FOLLOW, BECAUSE MANY FACTORS COME INTO PLAY. THE BEST WAY TO KNOW IF YOUR PLANT IS THIRSTY IS TO LOOK AT IT CLOSELY. BUT YOU SHOULD ALWAYS USE A FERTILIZER ON YOUR PLANT. DEADHEADING/PRUNING IS NOT VERY IMPORTANT FOR POTTED PLANTS.

What type of water should you use?

The best type of water contains some minerals (such as rainwater, spring, filtered, or mineral). It should also be slightly acidic (pH 6.5). Rainwater is always slightly acidic; for bottled water, read the label. You can also just use tap water. Add a little bit of citric acid to the water and let it sit for 24 hours to allow the chlorine to evaporate. If you have few plants, you can also use filtered water. Demineralized or osmosized water is good, but you will need to add a little liquid fertilizer, because they do not contain enough minerals. Dissolve the fertilizer in the water a few hours before watering.

Spray plants in the morning so that they are dry at night (this is when gas exchange in a plant is strongest and humidity can weaken the exchange). Never water when the sun is at its hottest or in very hot weather.

Green plants

• **Watering:** Watering needs depend on the species, the size and health of the plant, the size of the pot, the quality of the soil, the season, the ambient heat, the humidity of the room, and more. Water the plant if its leaves become less shiny or if it begins to sag a little, or if the pot is very light and sounds "hollow" when tapped. If the plant is really thirsty, it is better to water it several times at 10-minute intervals so that the soil is rehydrated gradually. Otherwise, the

GREEN PLANTS: EXTRA INFO

Since the air inside is drier than outside, use a small sprayer to mist the foliage of the plants several times a week.

The leaves are not washed by the rain inside, so shower your plants once a month under warm water, placing the container in a plastic bag to avoid getting soil everywhere.

Because the light only comes from one direction, the window, turn the pots each week by a quarter turn so that the plant will grow evenly.

water will flow directly around the sides of the parched root ball and the roots will not benefit. If necessary, soak the pot by immersing it in water for 15 minutes.

• **Fertilizer:** A potted plant needs fertilizer because continued watering can wash away the soil after a few months. It is better to use diluted doses (compared to what is recommended on the label) than to overdose the plant. Always use fertilizer granules or dilute the fertilizer in water before sprinkling onto damp soil.

• **Pruning:** This also depends on the species, but in general it is rare not to have to remove dried-out flowers or leaves that have turned brown. Do not rip off the dead leaves, though, or you could damage the plant. Use a pair of pruning shears instead.

Cacti and succulents

• **Watering:** People seem to think that cacti don't need watering. It is true that they are more likely to die from overwatering than from a lack of water, but like all plants, they still need some water to survive, especially potted cacti.

UNDERSTANDING WATER NEEDS

For all plants, water requirements are determined by several factors:

• The hotter and/or drier it is, the more often the plant will need water.

• The more light the plant receives, the more water it will need.

• A growing plant will need more water than a plant in a dormant state.

• Young plants will suffer more from a lack of water than older, well-established plants will.

• Rosette and fine-leaved plants require more water than more aerial or thick-leaved species.

As a general rule, you should repot a cactus every 2 to 3 years. Dust your plants with a brush and/or a hair dryer blowing cold air at a low flow rate.

- **Fertilizer:** From mid-April, add liquid fertilizer to the water every other watering. You can use cactus fertilizer, but if you do not have any, fertilizer for tomatoes or flowering plants, diluted by half, is suitable and less expensive. When the plant is in its dormant state, don't add fertilizer.
- **Pruning:** A lot of cacti don't require pruning. Some succulents, however, need to be thoroughly pruned so as not to become unmanageable. This is the case with *Crassula* species. They can be cut into small "trees" by pruning them regularly, ventilating among the branches, removing branches that intersect, and shortening them every 6 months so that they thicken instead of lengthen and don't bend under the weight of their thick foliage.

Orchids and air plants (tillandsias)

- **Watering:** Soak orchid pots in a bucket of water for 10 minutes every week or every 15 days in winter, when the roots have turned white. When the roots are bright green, it means they are well hydrated. For air plants, watering is done by spraying the leaves twice a week in the summer and once or twice every 10 to 12 days in the winter. Spraying is only effective if it is done generously. Wet the whole plant, top to bottom, 2 or 3 times at 5-minute intervals, to prevent the foliage from drying out too quickly and to give the plant time to absorb the water.
- **Fertilizer:** In nature, tillandsias feed on plant debris, water laden with mineral elements that trickles down the branches, or animal dung diluted by rainwater. Use orchid fertilizer

Cacti grow from spring to about mid-October. You should water them every 15 days. Start slowly, because too much water at any one time may burst their cells, which would result in necrosis (tissue death).

From mid-October to spring, they are in a dormant rest period. You should almost never water them during this period, unless they start to wilt. However, if the air inside the house is very dry, water them a little, at most once a month.

Only water when the soil is completely dry. Use water at room temperature and, if possible, use a little calcium carbonate (if your water is already alkaline, acidify it with a few drops of vinegar or lemon). Water the soil without wetting the cactus. To do this, remove the rose from the watering can and water the soil generously until the water starts to appear into the saucer under the pot. Wait 15 minutes, then empty the saucer.

Never water after repotting, as broken roots are sensitive to moisture, which increases the risk of rot. Give them some time to heal (7 to 10 days).

SOAKING ORCHIDS AND AIR PLANTS

Instead of misting, you can try immersing these plants in a bucket of water for a few minutes. Then you need to drain them before putting them back. Very scaly species, such as *Tillandsia usneoides* (Spanish moss), which are difficult to moisten properly with simple sprays, enjoy being soaked.

Soaking is also a good way to rehydrate these plants. This may be necessary if the leaves are curled up, forming a gutter shape. Allow your plant to soak for 2 or 3 hours in a bucket of water; you will see it come back to life before your very eyes.

at doses four times lower than those listed on the label, once or twice a month in the summer, once a month in the fall, and every other month in the winter. Always alternate watering with and without fertilizer in order to rinse the leaves and limit mineral deposits. Do not add fertilizer if it is too hot or if the plant is dehydrated or in bad shape.

• **Pruning:** Cut off the dry tips. Note that dry tips mean that the humidity is insufficient and that the frequency of misting should be increased.

AERATING TILLANDSIAS

Aeration is vital for air plants (in French, they are called "filles de l'air" or "air girls/daughters"). *Tillandsia juncea*, for example, will die quickly in a poorly ventilated room. Therefore, air plants can't be kept in terrariums for long amounts of time. To check if a plant is well ventilated, watch how fast it dries after being soaked in water: it should be completely dry within an hour. If it's not, move it.

10 ESSENTIAL CACTI AND SUCCULENTS

SOME CACTI WILL FIT IN WELL IN ANY ARRANGEMENT. THEY CAN BE FOUND EVERYWHERE, ALL YEAR ROUND; THEY DO NOT COST MUCH; AND THEY RESIST (ALMOST) EVERYTHING: DUMPING, POTTING, IRREGULAR WATERING, COMPETITION, ETC. HERE ARE OUR TOP TEN.

1. *Aloe variegata* (tiger aloe)
Tiger aloe looks great on windowsills, in the shade of other plants.

2. *Astrophytum myriostigma* (bishop's cap cactus)
These can take 4 years to flower, and they do so between April and October.

3. *Crassula ovata* (money plant)
This will live for many years, can reach the height of a man, and forms a thick trunk.

4. *Crassula perforata* (string of buttons)
A succulent, mid-sun plant that forms a tuft over time.

5. *Echinocactus grusonii* (golden barrel cactus)
In nature, this cactus can grow up to 10 ft. (3m) high. However, in a pot, it stays in a ball.

6. *Echeveria* sp.
The diversity of the foliage of the different species makes them addictive plants.

7. *Haworthia limifolia* (fairy washboard)
This succulent, closely related to aloe, prefers a subdued brightness.

8. *Kalanchoe tomentosa* (panda plant)
It can survive unprotected at a temperature of 28°F (-2°C) and, covered, it can survive at 19°F (-7°C) for short periods.

9. *Sempervivum* sp. (houseleek)
The large rosettes come in a variety of green and red shades, sometimes with red tips (as shown).

10. *Sedum album* (white stonecrop)
The stonecrop favors stony substrates.

Aloe variegata
ราคาพิเศษ

1
2
3
4
5
6
7
8
9
10

10 ESSENTIAL INDOOR PLANTS

THESE PLANTS ALL ENJOY PARTIAL SHADE, LIVE IN A LIMITED AMOUNT OF SOIL, GROW WELL, AND RESIST DISEASES AND PESTS. HERE IS OUR TOP TEN SELECTION, IDEAL FOR BEGINNERS AND WEEKEND GARDENERS.

1. *Ficus pumila* (creeping fig)
This creeping, fast-growing species is ideal for wet terrariums.

2. *Chirita* sp.
We love the blue, lavender, yellow, or white flowers, which depend on the variety.

3. *Chamaedorea elegans* (parlor palm)
It looks like a palm tree but flowers like a mimosa. It likes the shade.

4. *Chlorophytum comosum* (spider plant)
Its fleshy roots have the capacity to store water, so do not over-water it.

5. *Hoya carnosa* (wax plant)
Also known as the porcelain flower, this species needs at least 44 to 55°F (7 to 13°C) to grow well and bloom.

6. *Peperomia* sp. (radiator plant)
Radiator plants' leaves can absorb and store moisture from the air.

7. *Saintpaulia* sp. (African violet)
These violets require good soil and partial shade.

8. *Ficus benjamina* (weeping fig/ficus)
Grow as a bonsai, as a tree, with a spiral trunk, braided, with variegated foliage, etc.

9. *Tradescantia* sp. (spiderwort)
Drought, heat, humidity, hardship—these can resist everything, except slugs!

10. *Sansevieria* sp. (snake plant)
These requires very little care, little light, very little water, and little heat.

TERRARIUMS AND KOKEDAMAS

CREATING A MINI-FOREST FROM SCRATCH

WHAT YOU NEED

1 Chamaedorea excelsa

2 African violets

1 small variegated ficus (Ficus benjamina)

1 square glass jar

PLUS

1 piece of drainage felt

2 handfuls of clay balls

1 ¾ dry quarts / 8 ½ cups (2L) of potting soil

1 handful of moss

STEPS

1. Fill the jar with a 1" (3cm) layer of clay balls, the felt, and 2" (5cm) of potting soil. Pack it all in.

2. Immerse the plants for 1 minute and let them drain. Depot them and place them in the jar with the African violets around the outside.

3. Fill the empty spaces with potting soil, being sure to compact it.

4. Water the soil between the plants a little without soaking it. Place the moss on the surface.

WHEN?

All year.

CARE

Watering must be precise because there is no drainage; the soil must always remain moist, like a well-wrung sponge.

MINI-GREENHOUSES

WHAT YOU NEED

1 small cutting
of creeping fig
(*Ficus pumila*)

+

1 cutting of round
leaf peperomia
(*Peperomia rotundifolia*)

+

1 large jar about
8" (20cm) in diameter

PLUS

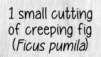

2 ¾ dry quarts / 12 ½ cups (3L)
of potting soil for green plants

1 handful of gravel

STEPS

1. Place a layer of gravel ¾" (2cm) deep at the base of the jar.

2. Add 4" (10cm) of soil.

3. Plant the cuttings (already rooted or not) with a spoon.
   Pack the soil in tightly around the stem or the roots.

4. Place a ¾" (2cm) layer of gravel on the surface.
   Water sparingly.

WHEN?

**All year long, since
the arrangement
is designed to
stay indoors.**

CARE

Make sure that no mold grows in the jar. Aerate it once a week for 1 to 2 hours.

A SMALL ECHEVERIA IN A JAR

WHAT YOU NEED

1 alpine eryngo
(*Eryngium alpinum*)
'Blue Star'

1 *Echeveria* sp.

1 eucalyptus branch

PLUS

1 round jar

1 handful of cacti potting soil

1 handful of clay balls

1 small mound of moss

STEPS

1. Place a layer of clay balls or gravel at the bottom of the jar. Put in a bit of soil.

2. Depot the echeveria. Drop a little soil in the jar, spread the plant's roots on top, and put some more soil over the roots.

3. Place the moss on the soil.

4. Decorate it with the eucalyptus and alpine eryngo.

WHEN?

All year. You can put the plants outside from May to September, in a place sheltered from the rain, but bright.

CARE

Water when the soil
is dry. Make sure it is
never soggy. If the soil is
soggy, take out the plants
and leave it to dry in
the fresh air.

A NATURE CORNER IN YOUR HOUSE

WHAT YOU NEED

1 young snake plant (*Sansevieria trifasciata*)

1 *Echeveria* 'Topsy Turvy'

1 cushion bush (*Leucophyta brownii*) (syn. *Calocephalus brownii*)

1 flared glass vase

PLUS

2 cups (0.5L) of gravel

4 ¼ cups (1L) of cacti potting soil

STEPS

1. Put a layer of gravel 1" (3cm) deep at the bottom of the vase.

2. Add 4" (10cm) of soil.

3. Place the plants and fill in with soil. Gently pack it all together with your fingers. Gently free the crowns of the plants from the surrounding soil.

4. Place ½" (1cm) of gravel on the surface to isolate the crowns of the plants from stagnant moisture.

WHEN?

All year. Keep the arrangement inside until mid-May. Put it outside in the shade during summer and bring it back inside by September.

CARE

Make sure that the soil is always slightly damp, but never too wet.

CREATING A GREEN AND WHITE FLOWERBED

WHAT YOU NEED

1 *Peperomia caperata*

+

1 air plant
(*Tillandsia* sp.)

+

2 white African
violets

+

1 maidenhair fern
(here *Adiantum
raddianum*)

PLUS

1 low-rimmed curved
glass container

White stone
gravel/pebbles

4 ½ dry quarts /
21 cups (5L) of
potting soil

1 handful of moss

STEPS

1. Immerse all the pots for 1 minute, drain, and remove the plants (with existing potting soil intact) from their pots..

2. Spread the soil along the bottom of the container to approximately a quarter the depth of the container. Place the plants.

3. Fill the empty space around the plants with potting soil, packing it in with your fingers.

4. Water the soil lightly before placing the moss on the surface. Decorate with white stone pebbles.

WHEN?

All year.

CARE

Remove faded or yellowing flowers and leaves. Water sparingly but regularly, since the container has no drainage holes.

AN AIR PLANT DISPLAY

WHAT YOU NEED

3 bottles

1 *Tillandsia ionantha 'Fuego'*

1 *Tillandsia gardneri*

Fine sand

Poppy seed pods

1 *Tillandsia lautneri*

1 wooden tray

STEPS

1. The day before creating this project, spray water on the air plants.

2. Place a bit of sand at the bottom of the bottles.

3. Put an air plant in each of the bottles. Re-cork the bottles.

4. Place the bottles on the tray and decorate it with the dried poppy seed pods.

WHEN?

All year.

CARE

Air plants need to be aerated, so this display is only temporary. You will need to take the plants out after about 24 hours.

A CUPFUL OF GREENERY

WHAT YOU NEED

1 pot of creeping
fig (*Ficus pumila*)

1 mound of moss

1 mini African violet

+

1 glass cup/container
of your choice

PLUS

2 cups (0.5L)
of river sand

1 ¾ dry quarts /
8 ½ cups (2L) of potting
soil for green plants

STEPS

1. Place a layer of sand at the bottom of the cup/container for drainage, then add potting soil.

2. Soak the plants for 1 minute, drain, and then depot them. Press them into the potting soil, which must be filled up to 2" (5cm) below the rim of the cup.

3. Water with a fine mist and avoid soaking the soil.

4. Finish by placing the moss.

WHEN?

All year.

CARE

Don't water the
African violet too much,
as it could rot if it has too
much water. Trim the
creeping fig when it
grows too big.

THE MEXICAN DESERT IN A JAR

WHAT YOU NEED

1 *Cereus* sp.
 +
2 small cacti
 +
1 large jar about 8" (20cm) in diameter

PLUS

2 cups (0.5L) of gravel

4 ¼ cups (1L) of cacti potting soil

STEPS

1. Spread at least 2" (5cm) of gravel along the bottom of the jar. Pour in 2" (5cm) of potting soil.

2. Depot the cacti. Place the plants on the soil and fill with gravel mixed with the soil.

3. Don't water the arrangement straight away. Wait 10 days, then take half a glass of water and pour it evenly over the plants.

WHEN?

All year long if you intend to keep the arrangement inside.

CARE

Place near a good light source but keep sheltered from the sun. Open the jar as often as possible. Water sparingly.

AIR PLANTS TAKE FLIGHT

WHAT YOU NEED

1 *Tillandsia gardneri*

+

1 *Tillandsia ionantha 'Fuego'*

+

1 *Tillandsia lautneri*

+

3 hanging ball-shaped mini-terrariums

PLUS

White sand

Some string

STEPS

1. The day before creating this project, spray water on the air plants. Hold them upside down to drain the water.
2. Pour a layer of sand about ½" (1cm) in depth along the bottom of the glass balls.
3. Put an air plant in each ball.
4. Hang in a well-ventilated place that is not too windy (the balls are quite fragile).

WHEN?

All year depending on your garden. These mini-terrariums in glass make pretty decorations for New Year's parties.

CARE
Take the plants out once a week and spray the leaves with water. Once a month, mix fertilizer in with the water.

LIGHTWEIGHT HANGING PLANTERS

WHAT YOU NEED

3 hanging ball-shaped mini-terrariums

1 young spider plant

1 small fern

Some stems of maidenhair

PLUS

Some string

1 handful of sand

2 cups (0.5L) of potting soil

STEPS

1. Put a mixture of soil and sand in the balls (two thirds soil, one third sand).

2. Plant the fern and the spider plant. Plant the strands of maidenhair. They are dotted with small rough spots where they take root very easily.

3. Pack the soil together with your fingers. Water sparingly.

4. Hang away from any air currents.

WHEN?

All year. You can put mini-terrariums in the garden or out on the terrace from May to September.

CARE

Watering is crucial because there isn't a lot of soil and it will dry out quickly. Water sparingly but regularly.

THE PERFECT KOKEDAMA FOR BEGINNERS

WHAT YOU NEED

1 mound of moss

1 small spider plant

2 cups (0.5L) of kokedama potting soil

Some green string

STEPS

1. Carefully depot the spider plant and shake the roots to make the existing soil fall off.

2. Shape a ball of kokedama soil around the roots, building up to a large ball of soil.

3. Add the moss and tie it up with the string.

4. Water under a tap, but keep the water flow light. Hang it up.

WHEN?

All year. The plant can be put outside from mid-May in a place sheltered from the wind.

CARE

Do not let the moss dry out. Spray it with mist every 2 days, more often in summer.

ORCHID KOKEDAMA

WHAT YOU NEED

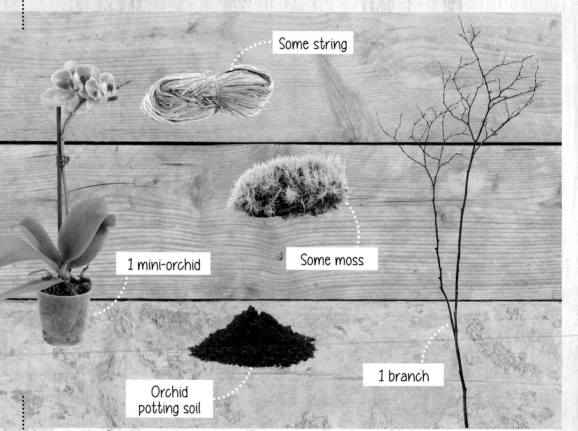

Some string

Some moss

1 mini-orchid

1 branch

Orchid potting soil

STEPS

1. Submerge the orchid pot in water for 1 minute. Depot the plant while trying to keep as much bark or substrate as possible around the roots.

2. Cover all the roots and bark with the slightly dampened moss, filling the inside with orchid soil as needed. Tie it all up with string.

3. Hang it on the branch.

4. Place in a room that isn't too sunny.

WHEN?

All year. Move to the garden when the orchid starts to bloom.

CARE

Spray mist on the moss once a week. If it is dry inside, dip the plant in water for 30 seconds every 15 days.

SUCCULENT KOKEDAMAS

WHAT YOU NEED

Different species
of echeveria

✛

Several branches

✛

Some moss

PLUS

✛

1 ball of green string

Kokedama potting soil

STEPS

1. Gently depot the echeverias and shake off the soil.

2. Shape a ball of kokedama soil around the roots of each echeveria.

3. Add the moss and tie it up with the string.

4. Water under a tap, but keep the water flow light. Hang on the branches.

WHEN?

All year, but if it is going outside, do it in April and make sure it gets enough light.

CARE

Water gently in the sink
whenever the moss is dry,
making sure the kokedama
does not fall apart.

GREEN WALLS

SPRING FORECAST

WHAT YOU NEED

4 already-sprouted
hyacinths

1 piece of beige
linen or burlap

Gold pushpins

4 half-gallon (2L) jars

3 yards (3m) of
thick string

PLUS

Adhesive labels

2 white
enamel jugs

1 small handful of
clay balls per pot

4 ½ dry quarts /
21 cups (5L) of
potting soil

1 handful of moss

STEPS

1. Put ¾" (2cm) of clay balls in each of the jars. Follow with ¾" (2cm) of soil.

2. Depot the hyacinths, put them in the jars, fill with soil, and compact it so that the bulbs are partially buried.

3. Glue a strip of linen/burlap on the glass. Write on the labels, then stick them on. Remove the tips of the pushpins with pliers and glue the golden heads at the corners of the labels.

4. Decorate the jars with moss. Attach the hanging strings. Hang alongside the jugs.

WHEN?

**In October if you want
to plant the bulbs. From
February if you have bought
already-sprouted plants.**

CARE

These need very little attention. Water once a week, more if it is very hot.

A DARING CACTUS SHELF

WHAT YOU NEED

3 aloes
(*Aloe vera*)

1 pincushion cactus
(*Mammillaria* sp.)

1 pincushion cactus
(*Mammillaria* sp.)

1 white shelf
with 9 spaces

1 *Cereus* sp.

1 *Cereus* sp.

2 hoyas
(*Hoya* sp.)

PLUS

Colored pots

Saucers

4 ½ dry quarts /
21 cups (5L) of sand +
4 ½ dry quarts /
21 cups (5L) of
potting soil for roses

OR

9 dry quarts /
42 cups (10L) of
cacti potting soil

STEPS

1. Repot each plant in pots of similar shapes and colors for overall harmony.

2. Use soil that is specially designed for cacti or make your own mix with half potting soil for roses and half not-too-fine sand.

3. Be careful not to damage the roots, as they are often quite fragile.

4. Put on the shelf. Wait a few days before watering.

WHEN?

All year.

CARE

Water sparingly once a week. Rotate each plant by a quarter turn every week.

STRAWBERRIES ON EVERY SHELF

WHAT YOU NEED

1 piece of drainage felt

3 rectangular zinc planters and their associated hanging fixtures

6 strawberry plants

1 slatted wooden panel

3 black mondo grass (Ophiopogon planiscapus 'Nigrescens')

18 dry quarts / 84 cups (20L) of potting soil

STEPS

1. Plant three strawberries each in two planters.
2. Plant the grass in the remaining planter.
3. Water the planters copiously and wait until they have finished draining.
4. Secure the panel to a wall, arranging the slats horizontally, and hang the planters.

WHEN?

In May and June. Later if your strawberry plants are already bearing fruit.

CARE

Don't let the soil dry out. Put fertilizer on the strawberry plants once a week and on the grass once a month.

A LITTLE PRIMROSE THEATER

WHAT YOU NEED

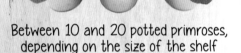

Between 10 and 20 potted primroses, depending on the size of the shelf

+

¼ gallon (1L) of wood paint

+

1 wooden shelf

PLUS

Between 10 and 20 terracotta pots

4 ½ dry quarts / 21 cups (5L) of potting soil for flowering plants

STEPS

1. Paint the shelf. Hang it in a cool, bright room, or outside, under a porch roof.

2. Soak each potted primrose in water for 1 minute. Repot them in terracotta pots.

3. Water them again and let them drain. Dry the bottoms of the pots.

4. Put them on the shelf.

WHEN?

From January or when they first appear in garden centers. Up to April or May.

CARE
Never let the soil dry out. Remove all faded and yellowing leaves as they appear.

CREATING A STUNNING FLORAL WALL

WHAT YOU NEED

4 pots of pelargoniums

4 pots of calibrachoas

Metal paint in whatever color you want

1 piece of drainage felt

9 dry quarts / 42 cups (10L) of potting soil for flowering plants

1 wooden plank

4 ¼ cups (1L) of clay balls

8 large cans

STEPS

1. Punch 2 holes in the bottom of each can. Paint them. Spread ½" (1cm) of clay balls, some felt, and ¾" (2cm) of potting soil in the bottoms of the cans.

2. Immerse the potted plants in a bucket of water for 1 minute. Depot them and put them into the cans.

3. Fill with potting soil and pack it all together with your fingers.

4. Water the plants and let them drain. Hang them on the plank.

WHEN?

From mid-May, when there is no risk of frost and when garden centers offer a wide array of plants and colors.

CARE

Water every 2 days, more if the pots are in the sun. Use liquid fertilizer once every 15 days, always on wet soil.

REPURPOSING VINTAGE OBJECTS

WHAT YOU NEED

1 green houseleek rosette with red tips and 2 green houseleek rosettes

1 vintage hammer

Pebbles

3 colored houseleek rosettes

1 vintage funnel

2 cups (0.5L) of potting soil

STEPS

1. Put some pebbles at the bottom of the funnel.
2. Fill it halfway with soil.
3. Plant the rosettes and fill the funnel with potting soil up to ½" (1cm) from the rim.
4. Water gently. Hang it up.
5. Add another vintage tool, such as a hammer, to complete the display.

WHEN?

Between March and September/October.

CARE

Water from time to time. Pick the new rosettes that form on the edges and transplant them elsewhere.

A LIVING WALL OF AIR PLANTS

WHAT YOU NEED

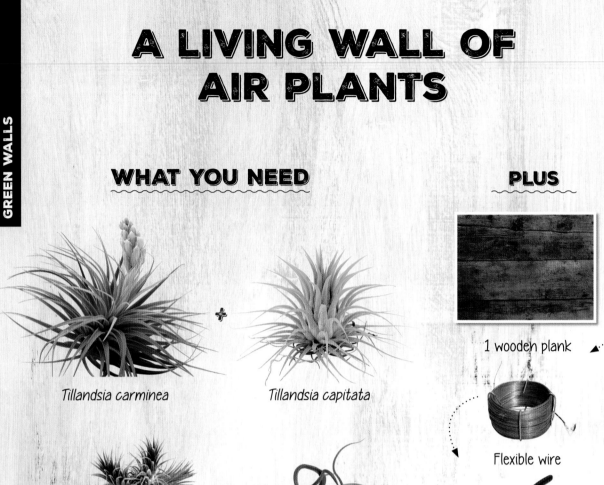

Tillandsia carminea + *Tillandsia capitata*

+ *Tillandsia tricholepis* + *Tillandsia bulbosa*

PLUS

1 wooden plank

Flexible wire

1 pair of pliers

1 hammer and some nails

STEPS

1. Let all the air plants sit in a bucket of warm water in which you have diluted a tiny dose of orchid fertilizer. Let the water drain.

2. Hammer as many nails in the board as there are plants, leaving at least 1" (2.5cm) of the nail exposed.

3. Wrap a thin, flexible wire around each plant.

4. Hang the plants one by one, grouping them however you want and passing the wire around the nails.

WHEN?

All year.

CARE

Once a week, spray the plants with warm water. Once a month, take them down and soak them in warm water for 5 minutes.

A BOTANICAL BIRDHOUSE

WHAT YOU NEED

PLUS

1 trash bag

Houseleek rosettes
(*Sempervivum* sp.)

Fine mesh

Sedum rosettes
(here *Sedum lucidum*)

1 stapler

Pink wood
paint

1 small handful
of gravel

1 birdhouse with raised roof
edges (not pictured), sometimes
called "green roof birdhouse"
or "living roof birdhouse"

4 ¼ cups (1L) of
potting soil

STEPS

1. If your birdhouse does not have raised roof edges, you can nail
   additional small wooden boards along the roofline to create the bed
   for the plants. Paint the birdhouse. Place a piece of the trash bag on one
   side of the roof and secure with a hammer and nails.

2. Fill one side of the roof with potting soil and gravel, then staple the
   wire mesh over the top of it. Place the rosettes into the potting soil,
   cutting a few stitches of the mesh to insert them through, and then
   fold the mesh back around the planted plants.

3. Do the same thing with the other side of the birdhouse roof.

WHEN?

**From February
to September.**

CARE

If a bird is nesting, leave the birdhouse alone. Otherwise, make sure that the thin layer of substrate does not dry out too soon.

PRIMROSES GROWING IN A SIEVE

WHAT YOU NEED

1 pot of primroses

1 vintage sieve

1 tin can

4 ¼ cups (1L) of potting soil

STEPS

1. Punch several holes in the bottom of the can with a drill or with a screwdriver and a hammer.

2. Repot the primrose in the can, taking care not to damage the root ball. Add additional soil as needed.

3. Water lightly, making sure all excess water can easily drain out of the base of the can.

4. Hang the sieve and place the primrose in it.

WHEN?

From March onward, when garden centers start to sell a wide range of different primroses.

CARE

Water regularly without soaking the soil. When the plant has lost its flowers, replant in the garden.

A LIVING WALL OF LETTUCE

WHAT YOU NEED

3 tin cans

10 yards (10m) of string

Lettuce plants

PLUS

1 piece of drainage felt

1 small handful of clay balls for each tin can

2 ¾ dry quarts / 12 ½ cups (3L) of potting soil

STEPS

1. Punch two holes in the bottom of each tin can.

2. Cut out 3 felt circles the same diameter as the cans.

3. Place ¾" (2cm) of clay balls at the bottom of each can, then a felt circle, then 2" (5cm) of potting soil.

4. Plant a lettuce plant in each can. Fill with soil and hang the cans up with string. Water them gently.

WHEN?

Between March and October. Sow new lettuce seeds every 15 days to replace the ones that you will inevitably eat.

CARE

Water very regularly.
Add a small amount
of organic fertilizer
every 15 days.

CREATIVE CONTAINERS

PUTTING SPRING IN BOXES

WHAT YOU NEED

1 pot of small yellow daffodils

+

1 empty can of olive oil in good condition

+

1 pot of small white double-headed daffodils

+

1 metal box in good condition

PLUS

1¾ dry quarts / 8½ cups (2L) of potting soil

STEPS

1. Punch several holes in the bottoms of the can and box.

2. Gently take each plant out of its pot without damaging the roots.

3. Plant each daffodil in one of the cans, being careful not to break the stems, which are often quite fragile.

4. Fill with soil and use a small stick to pack it in. Water a little bit.

WHEN?

From February, when daffodils start to sprout in garden centers.

A "LEEK"-ING TEAPOT

WHAT YOU NEED

1 pot of houseleeks
(or just the rosettes)

1 tin can

1 old teapot

PLUS

1 handful of clay balls

1 ¾ dry quarts / 8 ½ cups
(2L) of potting soil

STEPS

1. Punch 3 holes in the bottom of the tin can.
2. Put ½" (1cm) of clay balls at the bottom of the can and top it up with soil until it reaches three quarters full.
3. Plant the houseleeks in the can and fill with more soil. Water.
4. Put the can in the teapot. Place outside in the sun.

WHEN?

All year, but the best results are from March/April to September/October.

86

CARE
Even though houseleeks require little water, you need to water them from time to time, because there is not a lot of soil in this display.

BREATHE IN THE SEASIDE AIR

WHAT YOU NEED

1 pot
of lace aloe (*Aloe aristata*)

+

1 square glass jar

+

Some blue and green sand

PLUS

White sand

White stone gravel/pebbles

STEPS

1. Water the pot and let it drain.

2. Place the pot in the jar.

3. Fill the jar with colored and white sand, varying the thickness of the layers, up to about the halfway point.

4. Fill the rest of the space with white stone gravel/pebbles.

WHEN?
All year.

CARE

Water a little every 10 days. When the plant starts to spill out of its pot, move it to a bigger pot.

SUCCULENTS STRIKING A POSE

WHAT YOU NEED

Different sedums
(here *Sedum rupestre,
S. acre, S. pachyclados*)

+

1 pot of succulents
(*Sedum sp., Echeveria sp.*)

+

1 wooden
stepladder

PLUS

1 big
seashell

1 bowl

1 big handful
of clay balls

1 sieve

2 old cups

1 enamel
pitcher

2 ¾ dry quarts / 12 ½ cups
(3L) of cacti potting soil

STEPS

1. Punch holes in the bottoms of the containers that can be punched. Add ½" (1cm) of clay balls and ¾" (2cm) of soil.

2. Depot the succulents after a little watering, put them in their containers (line the sieve with felt), fill with soil, and pack it a little with your fingers to hold the plants in place. Water the plants a bit more.

3. Arrange the potted plants on the stepladder and decorate with knick-knacks.

WHEN?

From spring if the weather is pleasant. If not, wait until May.

CARE

Make sure tha
plants kept in a c
without holes ar
immersed in wate
them inside wh
starts to rair

LOVELY LOBELIAS IN A ROW

WHAT YOU NEED

1 tray of lobelias

PLUS

5 metal containers in bright colors

1 piece of drainage felt

3 handfuls of clay balls

2¾ dry quarts / 12½ cups (3L) of potting soil for flowering plants

STEPS

1. Punch holes in the bottoms of the containers. Spread ¾" (2cm) of clay balls, some felt, and 2" (4cm) of soil in the containers.

2. Submerge the lobelias in water for 1 minute. Let them drain, then depot them. Put the plants in the containers and fill with soil up to ½" (1cm) below the rim.

3. Pack everything in with your fingers, then gently water.

4. Put somewhere shady.

WHEN?
In May and June.

CARE

Water regularly (lobelias
don't like to be dry).
Add liquid fertilizer for
flowers every 15 days.

STRANGE-LOOKING HERMIT CRABS

WHAT YOU NEED

Some stems or cuttings of *Crassula tetragona*

Sea urchin shells

1 *Echeveria* sp.

Some stems or cuttings of *Crassula nudicaulis*

Some stems or cuttings of string-of-pearls (*Senecio rowleyanus*)

4 ¼ cups (1L) of cacti potting soil

STEPS

1. Put the stems or the cuttings in the openings of the sea urchin shells.
2. Gently fill with soil. Be careful, as the shells are very fragile
3. Using a thin stick, pack the soil in.
4. Water each plant with a gentle stream of water.

WHEN?

All year. At parties, these little ornaments make great placeholders.

CARE

Keep inside in a well-lit and not too busy place: the shells break very easily. Water every 10 days.

SPRING COMES EARLY

WHAT YOU NEED

10 snowdrop bulbs or 1 pot of already-sprouted snowdrops

1 handful of moss

PLUS

1 tin can

Some thick green wool

1 handful of clay balls

2 cups (0.5L) of potting soil

STEPS

1. Punch holes in the bottom of the can. Fill it with a ¾" (2cm) layer of clay balls, then fill it halfway with soil. Plant the bulbs and fill out with soil.

2. Leave the plant in the cold outside until you start to see shoots. Bring it back inside and wrap it in wool. Decorate it with moss.

3. Put it in a well-lit place and water every 5 days.

WHEN?

If you decide to use bulbs, plant them in September/ October. If you are using plants that have already sprouted, from January onward.

CARE

When the snowdrops start to wilt, replant them outside. They will grow again next year.

FUNNY-LOOKING OLIVES

WHAT YOU NEED

4 Haworthia cymbiformis

2 vintage metal containers

2 tin cans

1¾ dry quarts / 8½ cups (2L) of cacti potting soil

STEPS

1. Punch several holes in the bottoms of the metal containers and tin cans to allow for drainage.

2. Put a bit of soil at the bottom of each container.

3. Depot the succulents and put them in the containers. Fill with soil. Pack it together with your fingers.

4. Wait 3 days and water the plants lightly.

WHEN?

All year. You can put the plants outside between May and September, but keep them away from slugs.

Maçarico
WHOLE RIPE OLIVES

Net drained weight:
200 g = 7.0 oz
STERILIZED PRODUCT
PRODUCT OF PORTUGAL

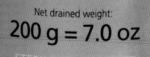

CARE
Water every week in summer without soaking the soil. Water once a month in winter.

MINERAL-ENHANCED PLANT

WHAT YOU NEED

1 French hydrangea
(*Hydrangea macrophylla*)

3 wooden blocks

White stone
gravel/pebbles

Some white stones

8 shower wall
hinges

4 pieces of shatterproof
glass, 15" x 15" (40 x 40cm)

2 ¾ dry quarts / 12 ½ cups
(3L) of potting soil

STEPS

1. Repot the hydrangea into a bigger pot, but one not more than 12" (30cm) in diameter.

2. Secure the 4 glass plates together with the hinges. Set on the ground.

3. Place the hydrangea on top of the wooden blocks in the middle of the glass assembly.

4. Fill the entire assembly with stones and then gravel/pebbles, including covering the top of the flowerpot with the gravel/pebbles.

WHEN?

Between April and September. Gravel has the advantage of insulating the pot against the cold.

CARE

Watering is complicated because it is hard to judge the state of the soil. Water at least once a week. Fertilize once a month.

VENTURE OFF THE BEATEN PATH

WHAT YOU NEED

1 century plant
(*Agave americana*)

Some houseleeks

10 pots of Scotch
moss (*Sagina sublata*)

Some cement

PLUS

18 dry quarts / 84 cups (20L)
of cacti potting soil

STEPS

1. Create a cement slab, leaving an irregular crevice 1 to 2 yards (1 to 2m) long and 4" to 20" (10 to 50cm) wide. Fill this cement crevice with soil to a depth of 12" (30cm).

2. Plant the agave in the largest part of the crevice. At its base, plant the Scotch moss, one plant every 12" (30cm) or so. In the remaining spaces, plant the houseleeks.

3. Level the soil and pack it all in with your hands.

4. Use a thin stream of water to water the plants and help the roots stick firmly in the soil.

WHEN?

In spring or summer.

CARE

Water the moss when the soil is dry to the touch. If the agave begins to spill out of the display, trim it with pruning shears.

FERNS,
A PIECE OF CAKE!

WHAT YOU NEED

1 old pastry tin/cake box

2 or 3 small potted ferns

1 piece of
drainage felt

2 ¾ dry quarts /
12 ½ cups (3L)
of potting soil

STEPS

1. Puncture holes along the bottom of the
   container. Line the inside with felt.

2. Fill it with soil to about a quarter of the way up.

3. Soak the plants for 1 minute, drain, and then
   depot. Put the plants in the container, fill it with
   soil, and pack it together with your fingers.

4. Water the ferns gently.

WHEN?

All year.

CARE

Keep the ferns in the shade and add fertilizer for green plants once a month. Don't let the soil dry out.

HYACINTHS ARE IN!

WHAT YOU NEED

Buds of hazel
in bloom

+

1 already-sprouted
hyacinth

+

1 glass vase

+

2 handfuls of moss

PLUS

Some quail eggs

1 raw beet or can of beets

STEPS

1. Hard boil the quail eggs in water and beet juice so that they turn pink. If you can't get quail eggs, buy artificial eggs and color them.

2. Put the potted hyacinth in the glass vase.

3. Cover up the pot with the moss.

4. Decorate with the branches and the eggs.

WHEN?

From October if using bulbs. From February if you bought a plant that has already sprouted.

CARE

Water the hyacinth sparingly. Remove any leaves or petals that have turned yellow.

A SUCCULENT GIFT BASKET

WHAT YOU NEED

Between 10 and 15 succulents, here lace aloe (*Aloe aristata*).

1 flat wooden tray

1 piece of drainage felt

3 ½ dry quarts / 17 cups (4L) of cacti potting soil

STEPS

1. Punch or drill holes in the bottom of the wooden tray. Spread the felt along the bottom, then pour in the potting soil.

2. Dip each plant in a bucket of water for 1 minute, drain, and depot.

3. Embed the plants in the soil and level it out, packing it together with your fingers.

4. Add more soil if necessary. Gently pack it all together with your fingers.

WHEN?

All year long, when succulents start to appear in garden centers.

CARE

Place the display near a well-lit window. Water the soil every 15 days, never watering the plants directly.

A LITTLE TASTE OF SUMMER ON YOUR WINDOW

WHAT YOU NEED

PLUS

3 tomato plants

+

2 trays of sprouts (any kind)

+

Aromatic herbs of your choice

+

Cardboard milk cartons or other containers

1 piece of drainage felt

+

1 shallow wooden crate or tray

+

Green paint

+

3 cans of tomatoes or tomato soup

2 ¾ dry quarts / 12 ½ cups (3L) of potting soil

STEPS

1. Repot each tomato plant into a tin can into which you have punched holes.

2. Cut the milk cartons to size and punch holes in the bottom. Plant the sprouts inside.

3. Paint words on the wooden crate with green paint. Line the crate with a piece of felt and arrange the potted herbs inside it.

4. Make sure that the soil is always moist but never soaking wet.

WHEN?

From early May, when the plants are available in garden centers and there is no risk of frost.

PLANTS

HYACINTHS IN A BOX

WHAT YOU NEED

2 hyacinth bulbs

+

1 vintage metal container

PLUS

1 piece of drainage felt

1 handful of clay balls

4 ¼ cups (1L) of potting soil

STEPS

1. Punch holes in the bottom of the container. Place ½" (1cm) of clay balls at the bottom. Then place a piece of felt that is the same size and shape of the container on top of the clay balls. Follow with ¾" (2cm) of soil. Plant the bulbs and cover with soil.

2. Put the display outside in a corner sheltered from the rain. Water lightly.

3. When the leaves start to wilt, you can bring the display back inside.

WHEN?

In October if you want to plant the bulbs. From February if you have bought already-sprouted plants.

CARE

Keep the soil slightly
damp over winter. Water
a little more if the
flowers start to wilt.

SUCCULENT UPHOLSTERY

WHAT YOU NEED

Different green, silver, and pink echeverias

1 chair

Marine blue plywood

PLUS

1 piece of drainage felt

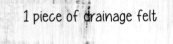

1 ¾ dry quarts / 8 ½ cups (2L) of potting soil

Some pebbles

STEPS

1. Remove the seat of the chair and cut a piece of plywood the shape and size of the seat. Drill drainage holes 8" (20cm) apart on the plywood piece.

2. Attach the plywood onto the chair seat from below. Add the felt on top.

3. Depot the plants and plant them on top of the seat, packing soil around them.

4. Water and top the soil with the pebbles.

WHEN?

From May, when you can start putting chairs outside. All year in places with a warm climate.

CARE

Make sure the plants are well watered. Bring back inside before the frost starts again.

POTS AND PLANTERS

TREAT YOURSELF TO SOME SPRINGTIME SWEETS

WHAT YOU NEED

1 cutting of inch plant
(*Tradescantia zebrina*)

Some branches
of pussy willow

PLUS

1 distressed cream-
colored planter

1 piece of
drainage felt

2 cups (0.5L) of clay balls

4 ½ dry quarts / 21 cups
(5L) of potting soil

STEPS

1. Soak the inch plant for 2 minutes in a bucket of water. Drain and depot.

2. At the bottom of the planter, place ¾" (2cm) of clay balls, a piece of felt, and 3" (8cm) of potting soil. Pack it all in.

3. Plant the inch plant and fill with soil. There should be ¾" (2cm) of empty space under the rim.

4. Water gently. Put the branches in a vase next to the planter.

WHEN?

From March, when catkins start to grow.

CARE

Only water when the ground is dry to a depth of 1¼" (3cm). Cut the plant if it becomes too big, and use the cuttings to grow new plants.

ORANGE IS THE NEW GREEN

WHAT YOU NEED

1 orange metal basin

1 parsley plant

2 handfuls of clay balls

1¾ dry quarts / 8 ½ cups (2L) of potting soil

1 piece of drainage felt

STEPS

1. Puncture holes in the bottom of the basin. Put ¾" (2cm) of clay balls at the bottom of the basin, then a piece of felt, then 2" (5cm) of soil.

2. Soak the parsley for 2 minutes in water, drain, depot, and plant in the soil.

3. Fill in around the plant with soil and compact it.

4. Water gently.

WHEN?

Between March and September. Sow more parsley every 3 weeks to keep the display looking green.

CARE

Keep well lit.
Pick the parsley
regularly. Never let
the soil dry out.

A WATERFALL OF GREEN

WHAT YOU NEED

1 low bulrush
(*Scirpus cernuus*)

+

2 string-of-pearls
(*Senecio rowleyanus*)

+

1 bowl

+

1 high stand

PLUS

1 piece of
drainage felt

3 handfuls of clay balls

4 ½ dry quarts / 21 cups
(5L) of potting soil

STEPS

1. Drill holes in the bottom of the bowl if it does not already have them. Add ¾" (2cm) of clay balls, some felt, and 1¼" (3cm) of soil.

2. Soak the potted plants in a bucket of water. Depot them. Put the plants in the bowl. Fill around them with soil.

3. Starting at the edges, compact the soil (this will stabilize the plants).

4. Add more soil as needed until the soil level is about ¾" (2cm) below the rim of the bowl. Water gently. Place in a well-lit room.

WHEN?

All year long, depending on when indoor plants first appear in your local garden centers.

CARE
Water every week, always on the low bulrush and not on the string-of-pearls. Add fertilizer once a week.

TRAVELING TO HOT CLIMATES

WHAT YOU NEED

1 mother of millions with fine leaves (here *Kalanchoe. tubliflora*)

+

1 *Haworthia fasciata*

+

1 living stone (*Lithop* sp.)

+

1 bishop's cap cactus (*Astrophytum myriostigma*)

+

1 silver ruffles (*Cotyledon undulata*)

+

1 *Ferocactus histrix*

1 square terracotta pot

PLUS

2 handfuls of gravel

1¾ dry quarts / 8½ cups (2L) of cacti potting soil

STEPS

1. Put 1¼" (3cm) of gravel at the bottom of the pot (make sure the pot has holes in it). Then pour the soil on top.

2. Put in the plants and fill with soil up to about 1½" (4cm) below the rim.

3. Pack the soil together with your fingers.

4. Finish by spreading a ½" (1cm) layer of gravel along the top of the soil. This layer of gravel will protect the crowns of the plants from humidity and possible root rot in winter.

WHEN?

All year. You can put the plants outside from May to September, in a place sheltered from the rain, but bright.

CARE

Make sure that the soil has dried out before watering again. In May, you can put the display outside, sheltered from the wind.

IN LIFE, THERE ARE CACTI

WHAT YOU NEED

PLUS

1 can of white spray paint

2 ¾ dry quarts / 12 ½ cups (3L) of cacti potting soil

2 cups (0.5L) of white gravel

1 *Echinopsis* sp.

1 old man cactus (*Cephalocereus senilis*)

1 *Ferocactus histrix*

1 metal basin

STEPS

1. Spray paint the basin white. Let it dry. Put 1¼" (3cm) of gravel at the bottom. Then pour soil on top.

2. Put in the plants and fill with soil up to about 1½" (4cm) below the rim.

3. Pack the soil together with your fingers.

4. Spread ½" (1cm) of gravel on the top of the soil.

WHEN?

All year. You can put the plants outside from May to September, in a place sheltered from the rain, but bright.

CARE

Water every 15 days, always at the base (never pour water directly onto the cacti). Fertilize the cacti every 2 months between April and September.

A NEAT MANICURE FOR YOUR SNAKE PLANT

WHAT YOU NEED

2 white or translucent pots

1 paintbrush

Masking tape

White water-based paint

1 ¾ dry quarts / 8 ½ cups (2L) of cacti potting soil

2 cylindrical snake plants (*Sansevieria cylindrica*)

Some moss

STEPS

1. Repot each plant in a white or translucent pot.
2. Put the moss around the base of each plant. Wrap the plants with masking tape 4" (10cm) from the ends.
3. Paint the tips above the tape with white paint.
4. Carefully remove the tape before the paint dries.

WHEN?

All year, depending on your garden center.

CARE

Water the plants sparingly. Rotate the plants by a quarter turn every week.

AN ADORABLE DRY MINI-GARDEN

WHAT YOU NEED

1 Eve's pin
(*Austrocylindropuntia*)
subulata

+

1 tiger aloe (*Aloe variegata*)

+

1 *Echeveria* sp.

+

1 money plant
(*Crassula oyata*)

PLUS

+

1 metal basin

1 can of white spray paint

3 ½ dry quarts / 17 cups (4L) of cacti potting soil

4 ¼ cups (1L) of white gravel

STEPS

1. Spray paint the basin. Let it dry. Put 1¼" (3cm) of gravel at the bottom. Then pour some soil on top.

2. Put in the plants and fill around them with soil up to about 1½" (4cm) below the rim.

3. Pack the soil together with your fingers.

4. Finish with a layer of gravel ½" (1cm) deep on top of the soil.

WHEN?

All year. You can put the plants outside in a well-lit place that is sheltered from the rain from May to September.

CARE

Make sure that there is
no stagnant water at the
bottom of the basin. Cut
back the money plant if
it starts to suffocate
the other plants.

MOSS UP YOUR DÉCOR!

WHAT YOU NEED

PLUS

1 piece of drainage felt

2 handfuls of clay balls

2 metal containers

2 pots of helxine
(*Soleirolia soleirolii*)

1 ¾ dry quarts / 8 ½ cups
(2L) of potting soil

STEPS

1. Soak the plants for 1 minute, drain, and then depot them.
2. Make sure that the containers have holes at the bottom. Put ½" (1cm) of clay balls at the bottom, then the felt, then about 1½" (4cm) of soil. Place the plants.
3. Fill in around the plants with soil and pack in around the edges.
4. Water gently so that the soil will stick to the roots.

WHEN?

All year long, but preferably in spring, because helxine grows better outside than in.

CARE

Water regularly. Trim back the helxine with a pair of scissors when it starts to get out of control.

A LOVELY COLLECTION OF CACTI

WHAT YOU NEED

1 *Echinocereus* sp.

1 *Ferocactus histrix*

1 chin cactus
(*Gymnocalycium* sp.)

1 old man cactus
(*Cephalocereus senilis*)

1 *Echinopsis* sp.

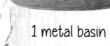

1 metal basin

PLUS

3 ½ dry quarts / 17 cups
(4L) of cacti potting soil

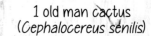

4 ¼ cups (1L)
of white gravel

STEPS

1. Put 1¼" (3cm) of gravel at the bottom of the basin. Then pour in some soil.

2. Put in the plants and fill with soil up to about 1½" (4cm) below the rim.

3. Pack the soil together with your fingers.

4. Finish by adding a layer of gravel ½" (1cm) deep on top of the soil.

WHEN?

All year. You can put the plants outside in a well-lit place that is sheltered from the rain from May to September.

CARE
Make sure that there is no stagnant water at the bottom of the basin. Water sparingly.

NASTURTIUMS GET A MAKEOVER

WHAT YOU NEED

3 pots of nasturtiums

1 large cage

1 piece of drainage felt

Clay balls

2 ¾ dry quarts / 12 ½ cups (3L) of potting soil

1 pot, 10" (25cm) in diameter

STEPS

1. Put ¾" (2cm) of clay balls at the bottom of the pot, then the felt, followed by 2" (5cm) of soil.

2. Depot the plants, plant them in the soil and fill with more soil, then pack it all together with your fingers.

3. Water gently. Put the pot in the cage, feeding the stems gently through the bars.

WHEN?

If you buy already-sprouted plants, put them out at the start of May. If you sow them yourself, plant them at the end of March.

CARE
Water very regularly. Add fertilizer for flowering plants every 15 days.

SIMPLY EASY SUCCULENTS

WHAT YOU NEED

 +  +  +

2 pots of crassula
(here *C. ovata*
and *C. arborescens*
'Undulatifolia')

2 pots of
Echeveria sp.

2 pots of helxine
(*Soleirolia soleirolii*)

6 terracotta pots

PLUS

+

1 crate, split into
6 compartments

1 small handful of clay
balls for each pot

4 ½ dry quarts /
21 cups (5L) of
potting soil

STEPS

1. Submerge each pot in water for 1 minute. Let them dry, and then depot.

2. Repot each plant in a new terracotta pot.

3. Trim the helxines if they are too large compared to the other plants.

4. Put each potted plant in a different compartment of the crate.

WHEN?

All year. You can put the
display outside between
May and October.

CARE
Trim the helxine regularly. Water the succulents sparingly.

PLANT INDEX

A

Adiantum raddianum ✎ 42
African violet ✎ 34, 46
African violet (white) ✎ 42
Agave americana ✎ 102
Air plant (Tillandsia sp.) ✎ 42, 44, 50, 74
Aloe (Aloe vera) ✎ 64
Aloe aristata ✎ 88, 108
Aloe variegata ✎ 28-29, 130
Aloe vera ✎ 64
Alpine eryngo (Eryngium alpinum 'Blue Star') ✎ 38
Aromatic herbs ✎ 110
Astrophytum myriostigma ✎ 28-29, 124
Austrocylindropuntia subulata ✎ 130

B

Bishop's cap cactus (Astrophytum myriostigma) ✎ 28-29, 124
Black mondo grass (Ophiopogon planiscapus 'Nigrescens') ✎ 66

C

Calibrachoa ✎ 70
Calocephalus brownii ✎ 40
Century plant (Agave americana) ✎ 102
Cephalocereus senilis ✎ 126, 134
Cereus sp. ✎ 48, 64
Chamaedorea elegans ✎ 30-31
Chamaedorea excelsa ✎ 34
Chin cactus (Gymnocalycium sp.) ✎ 134
Chirita sp. ✎ 30-31
Chlorophytum comosum ✎ 30-31
Cotyledon undulata ✎ 124
Crassula (C. ovata and C. arborescens 'Undulatifolia') ✎ 138
Crassula arborescens 'Undulatifolia' ✎ 138
Crassula nudicaulis ✎ 94
Crassula ovata ✎ 28-29, 130, 138
Crassula perforata ✎ 28-29
Crassula tetragona ✎ 94
Creeping fig (Ficus pumila) ✎ 30-31, 36
Cushion bush (Leucophyta brownii) ✎ 40

D

Double-headed white daffodil ✎ 84

E

Echeveria ✎ 38, 40
Echeveria sp. ✎ 28-29, 38, 90, 94, 114, 130, 138
Echeveria 'Topsy Turvy' ✎ 40
Echinocactus grusonii ✎ 28-29
Echinocereus sp. ✎ 134
Echinopsis sp. ✎ 126, 134
Eryngium alpinum 'Blue Star' ✎ 38
Eucalyptus (branch) ✎ 38
Eve's pin (Austrocylindropuntia subulata) ✎ 130

F

Fern ✎ 52, 104
Ferocactus histrix ✎ 124, 126, 134
Ficus benjamina ✎ 30-31
Ficus benjamina (variegated) ✎ 34
Ficus pumila ✎ 30-31, 36
Ficus pumila (variegated) ✎ 46
French hydrangea (Hydrangea macrophylla) ✎ 100

G

Gymnocalycium sp. ✎ 134

H

Haworthia cymbiformis ✎ 98
Haworthia fasciata ✎ 124
Haworthia limifolia ✎ 28-29
Hazel (buds) ✎ 106
Helxine (Soleirolia soleirolii) ✎ 132, 138
Houseleek (Sempervivum sp.) ✎ 28-29, 86, 102
Hoya carnosa ✎ 30-31
Hoya sp. ✎ 64
Hyacinth ✎ 62, 106
Hyacinth (bulbs) ✎ 112
Hydrangea macrophylla ✎ 100

I

Inch plant (*Tradescantia zebrina*) 118

K

Kalanchoe tomentosa 28-29
Kalanchoe tubliflora 124

L

Lace aloe (*Aloe aristata*) 88, 108
Lettuce 80
Leucophyta brownii (syn.
    Calocephalus brownii) 40
Lithop sp. 124
Living stone (*Lithops* sp.) 124
Lobelia 92
Low bulrush (*Scirpus cernuus*) 122

M

Maidenhair 52
Maidenhair fern (*Adiantum raddianum*)
    42
Mammillaria sp. 64
Money plant (*Crassula ovata*) 28-29,
    130, 138
Mother of millions (*Kalanchoe tubliflora*)
    124

N

Nasturtium 136

O

Old man cactus (*Cephalocereus senilis*)
    126, 134
Ophiopogon planiscapus 'Nigrescens' 66
Orchid (mini) 56

P

Parsley 120
Pelargonium 70
Peperomia caperata 42
Peperomia rotundifolia 36
Peperomia sp. 30-31
Pincushion cactus (*Mammillaria* sp.) 64
Primrose 68, 78
Pussy willow (branches) 118

R

Round leaf peperomia (*Peperomia
    caperata*) 42

S

Sagina sublata 102
Saintpaulia sp. 30-31
Sansevieria cylindrica 128
Sansevieria sp. 30-31
Sansevieria trifasciata 40
Scirpus cernuus 122
Scotch moss (*Sagina sublata*) 102
Sedum 28-29, 76, 90
Sedum acre 90
Sedum album 28-29
Sedum lucidum 76
Sedum pachyclados 90
Sedum rupestre 90
Sedum sp. 90
Sempervivum sp. 72, 76
Senecio rowleyanus 42, 94, 122
Silver ruffles (*Cotyledon undulata*) 124
Snake plant (*Sansevieria* sp.) 30-31
Snowdrop (bulb) 96
Soleirolia soleirolii 132, 138
Spider plant 30-31, 52, 54
Sprouts 110
Strawberry 66
String-of-pearls (*Senecio rowleyanus*)
    94, 122

T

Tiger aloe (*Aloe variegata*) 28-29, 130
Tillandsia bulbosa 74
Tillandsia capitata 74
Tillandsia carminea 74
Tillandsia gardneri 44, 50
Tillandsia ionantha 'Fuego' 44, 50
Tillandsia lautneri 44, 50
Tillandsia sp. 42
Tillandsia tricholepis 74
Tomato 110
Tradescantia sp. 30-31
Tradescantia zebrina 118

W

Weeping fig (*Ficus benjamina*) 30-31, 34

Y

Yellow daffodil 84

IMAGE CREDITS

Abbreviations used: **b = bottom, r = right, l = left, m = middle, t = top.**

Olivier Ploton © Archives Larousse : soil, felt, clay balls, gravel.

© Biosphoto : Agnes Kantaruk/Flora Press 39, Georgie Steeds/Flora Press 79, Nadja Buchczik/ Flora Press 85, Caroline Burek/Flora Press 97, Flora Press/Flora Press 99, Otmar Diez/Flora Press 111, Visions Pictures 122lt (low bulrush).

© Catherine Delvaux : 66 (ophiopogon), 101.

© DR 50 (mini-terrarium), 52 (terrarium), 100 (hinge).

© Fotolia : Lengebaka 34 (chamaedorea), Smspsy 34 (ficus l), Ekarin 36 (gravel), Marinkin 38 (jar), Tamara Kulikova 38 (eucalyptus), Smspsy 38 (eryngium), Xiaoliangge 38 (echeveria), Tapaton 38 (moss), Dizolator 40 (vase), Ekarin 40 (gravel), Arayabandit 44 (plate), Ekarin 48 (gravel), Premkh 50 (string), Richard Griffin 52 (fern), Unclesam 56 (string), Ortis 56 (branches), Xiaoliangge 58 (echeveria), Richpav 62 (hyacinth), Onairjiw 62 (linen canvas), Beckystarsmore 62 (jar), Premkh 62 (string), Kwangmoo 62 (label), Spinetta 64 (aloe), Petr Malyshev 66 (tray), Hayati Kayhan 76 (birdhouse), Olaola 86 (teapot), Coprid 88 (white sand), M. Schuppich 90 (sedums), Vidady 90 (succulents), Marek Walica 90 (stepladder), Sytilin 90 (cup), Petrov Vadim 90 (bowl), Karandaev 90 (jug), Byron Ortiz 90 (shell), Comugnero Silvana 90 (sieve), Ivonne Wierink 92 (lobelia), Richard Griffin 100 (hydrangea), Simic Vojislav 102 (leek), Joloei 104 (ferns), Dizolator 106 (vase), Sb goodwin 108 (aloe tl), Mosstan 108 (aloe tr), Sasimota 108 (box), Stock photo 110 (aromatics), Alter_photo 100 (cage), akepong srichaichana 110 (seeds), Xiaoliangge 114 (echeveria), Ekarin 114 (pots), Olsio 118 (inchplant), Pitakareekul 124 (ferocactus), Timfeev 128 (paint), Kungverylucky 128 (pliers), Smspsy 130 (echeveria), Nikolay N. Antonov 130 (austrocylindropuntia), Meliac 132 (helxine), Simic Vojislav 138 (crassula), Smspsy 138 (echeveria), Melica 138 (helxine), Salamahin 138 (pot), Cretolamna 138 (box).

© GAP Photos : Bureaux 35, 37, 41, Bureaux 43, Visions 45, Jerry Pavia 37/47, 49, Visions 51, 53, FhF Greenmedia 55, Visions 57, Visions 59, Visions 63, Matteo Carassale 65, J S Sira 67, Juliette Wade 69 & 71, 73, Bureaux 75, 77, 81, Nicola Stocken 87, Clive Nichols 89, Julia Boulton 91, Victoria Firmston 93, Brent Wilsons 95, Rob Whitworth 103, Visions 105, Juliette Wade 107, Andrea Jones 109, Nicola Stocken 113, 115, Visions 119, Clive Nichols 121, Elizabeth Mercer 123, 125, Visions 127, 129, 131, 133 & 135, Nicola Stocken 137, Juliette Wade 139.

© Shutterstock : Choti Pavel 6-7, Getideaka (background) & Lechernica (drawings) 10-11, Vakhrushev 12bl, oksanaBgu 12br, archideaphoto 13t, Shaiith 13m, Stanislav71 14, Diana Taliun 15t, Wavebrakmedia 15b, Yada 16t, Kathy Burns 16m, Richard Griffin 16b, EstlanPhot 17t, Africa Studio 17m, Alekseykolotvin 17b, sanddebeautheil 18m, Daria Minaeva 18bl, rattiya lamrod 18br, Coprid 19tr, Paul Triska 19b, sukiyaki 20bl, luckyshoe 20br, imnoom 21, IgorAleks 22bl, vasara 22mr, Polina Letshina 23, Robert Przybysz 24t, Lipik Stock Media 24b, Photographee.eu 25t, Design Exchange 25b, nafterphoto 26t, Agnes Kantaruk 26b, patchii 27t, Noppharat888 27tr, Piti Tan 27b, alchemist 28-29 n°1, Lttipon 28-29 n°2, svf74 28-29 n°3, Jessicahyde 28-29 n°4, Praiwun Thungsarn 28-29 n°5, Simon Tang 28-29 n°6, nattapan72 28-29 n°7, White Tulip 28-29 n°8, BeppeNob 28-29 n°9, NatalkaDe 28-29 n°10, Jack Photographer 30-31 n°1, Shihina 30-31 n°2, RomBo 64 30-31 n°3, Bozhenz Melnyk 30-31 n°4, PavelKant 30-31 n°5, nmoktp 30-31 n°6, Kosobu 30-31 n°7, Ina Ts 30-31 n°8, Phatthanun Kaewsuwan 30-31 n°9, karimpard 30-31 n°10, nafterphoto 32, fffffly 33, Pavel Aleks 34 (jar), GlandStudio 36 (ficus), JIANG HONGYAN 36 (peperomia), Epitavi 40 (sansevieria), Christina Siow 40 (echeveria), Icrms 40 (leucophyta), 31moonlight31 42 (plate), Andrew Mayovskyy 42 (peperomia), Sanit Fuangnakhon 42 (tillandsia), Vitasunny 42 (African violet), Sanit Fuangnakhon 44tl (tillandsia), Kamnuan 44tm (tillandsia), Konstantins Pobilojs 44bm (tillandsia), Hot ice 44 (sable), Diana Taliun 44 (poppy), Natu 46 (ficus), Alexandrova Elena 46 (African violet), V.gi 46 (cup), Spkphotostock 48 (cactus), Kamnuan 50tm (tillandsia), Sanit Fuangnakhon 50tl (tillandsia), YamabikaY 50 (white sand), Modest Things 52 (maidenhair), Eakkachai halang 52 (string), Vesna Cvorovic 58 (branch), GoodMood Photo 60l, Julia Roshchina 60m, LAVENTEVA 61, FWStudio 64 (cactus/4 ph.), OKsarra Shufrych 64 (shelf), AfricaStudio 64 (blue pot), Luchi-a 64 (black pot), Sunny_baby 68 (primroses), Maik Kirsten 72 (funnel), Sanit Fuangnakhon 74tl (tillandsia), Areeya-ann 74tm (tillandsia), Kamnuan 74bl (tillandsia), Hawk777 74bm (tillandsia), Matteo Giotto 74 (iron wire), Imstock 74 (hammer and nails), Freer 76 (sedum), Mutation 78 (screen), Anastasia Potapova 82, Alenka Karabanova 83, Sarycheva Olesia 84 (white daffodil), Wegosi 88 (box), Urbanbuzz 88 (basin), Gavran333 86 (houseleek), Tony Stock 86 (box), Africa Studio 88 (aloe), Pavel Aleks 88 (jar), RedNumberOne 88 (blue sand), Dutch Scenery 92 (box), Gowithstock 94tl (crassula), Fabrika Simf 94bl (crassula), 54613 94 (senecio), JIB Liverpool 98 (haworthia), antonSov85 98 (box), boghey 100 (cales), rangizzz 100 (plates), Thomas Soellner 102 (cement), Egor Rodynchenko 106 (beetroot), Chrisdorney 110 (box), Sergey85 110 (milk), motorolka 114 (haworthia), DalDaFoTo 116, Agenk Restyamaji 117, Zerbor 120 (parsley), Irinak 122 (senecio), Martina-L 122 (cup), lady-luck 122 (support), Tawin Mukdharakosa 124 (astrophytum), Eric Isselee 124 (cotyledon), Unkas Phob 124 (lithop), Motorolka 124 (pot), Doadhor 124 (kalanchoe), Onair 124 (haworthia), Kolpakova Daria 126 (cepholocerus), Zoran Orcik 126 (echinopsis), Triff 126 (ferocactus), bogdan ionescu 126 (gravel), Bega 128 (sansevieria), AE Panuwat Studio 130 (crassula), Ekaterina Lin 130 (aloe), bogdan ionescu 130 (gravel), Watcharaporn Noisakul 134 (gymnocalycium), Zoran Orcik 134 (echinopsis), Éric Isselee 134 (cephalocereus & echinocereus), bogdan ionescu 134 (gravel), Kitch Bain 136 (pot), Vakhrushev 144.

© **Thinkstock :** Adisa 34 (African violet), Fotek 34 (moss), Stargalechnis 36 (jar), Nasico 36 (soil), Nasico 40 (soil), Kf4851 42 (fern), natthanim 42 (stone chips), Akiyoko 44 (bottle), Fotek 46 (moss), Stargalechnis 48 (jar), Nito100 48 (cactus), Nasico 48 (soil), ElenaMirage 52 (spider plant), ElenaMirage 54 (spider plant), Fotek 54 (moss), Potapenkoi 54 (string), Nasico 54 (soil), Fotek 56 (moss), Amor_Kar 56 (orchid), Fotek 58 (moss), Potapeukol 58 (string), Chet_W 62 (pushpins), Antagain 64 (hoya), Vikif 64 (saucers), Aguirre-mar 66 (strawberry), PhonlamaiPhoto 66 (planter), Kazoka30 68 (paint pot), Scisettiafio 68 (pot), Tentan 68 (shelf), Thawomnurak 70 (plank), Simic Vojislav 70 (pelargonium), bazilfoto 70 (calibrachoa), Scanrail 70 (paint pots), Wavebrakmedia Ltd 70 (box), Pjhpx 72 (houseleek red), Gavran333 72 (houseleek green), Nasico 72 (soil), phanasitti 72 (hammer), Karp5 74 (plank), Zoonar RF 74 (pliers), Gavran333 76 (houseleeks), Thawats 76 (mesh), Imagehub88 76 (paint), Tevarak 76 (stapler), PitakAreekul 78 (box), Seg_ Velusceac 78 (primrose), Wavebrakmedia Ltd 80 (box), Toxitz 80 (string), Hydrangea100 80 (lettuce), Wavebreakmedia Ltd 84 (yellow daffodil), Natthanim 88 (stone chips), Hanohiki 94 (echeveria), Buxtree 94 (sea urchin), eAlisa 94 (hyacinth), mongkol_sorasit 96 (snowdrop bulbs), _Vilor 96 (snowdrop), Wavebrakmedia Ltd 96 (box), Olga_Danylenko 96 (wool), Fotek 96 (moss), mm88 98 (tin), Thousandies 102 (agave), Arnaud Weisser 102 (sagine), Bob Wes 104 (box), Multik7 106 (hazel tree), Kazakovmaksim 106 (hyacinth), Tamara_kulikova 106 (quail eggs), Fotek 106 (moss), Cynoclub 110 (plants), Kazoka30 110 (paint pots), Kazakovmaksim 112 (hyacinth), Hemera Technologies 112 (box), Bigpra 114 (plywood), Gameover2012 114 (chair), DykyoStudio 118 (container), Hallgerd 118 (branches), Ajt 120 (container), MitchelRaman 124 (gravel), Grasetto 126 (spray), Sergeyskleznev 126 (basin), VIP DesignUSA 128 (planter), Antpkr 128 (tape), Sergeyskleznev 130 (basin), Iserg 132 (container), Brand x Pictures 134 (ferocactus), Sergeyskleznev 134 (basin), FotoZlaja 136 (nasturtium), Margo JH 136 (cage).

Catherine Delvaux, agricultural engineer, is editor-in-chief of the French magazine *Détente jardin* [Relaxing garden] and author of numerous gardening titles, including titles on garden projects, vegetable gardens, gardening techniques, ecological gardening, and organic gardening. She is also a contributor to *Le Truffaut*, a prestigious French gardening encyclopedia.